The Joyful Mother Promise

A 7-Day Devotional

ELIZABETH WILSON

Nova Sei

P R E S S

It's time to receive
The Joyful Mother Promise.

INTRODUCTION

We live in a time when many call infertility, barrenness, miscarriages, and stillbirths "normal." Yet, the Word of God has not changed, and the Lord has not changed His mind, His will, or His plan.

> He maketh the barren woman to keep house, and to be a joyful mother of children. Praise ye the Lord.
> —Psalm 113:9 (KJV)

Regardless of the situation you face, or the fear the devil tries to plague you with, the Lord chose you to live in this hour. That means He has grace for you to overcome any challenges or obstacles, and He offers you wisdom to navigate whatever comes your way. He is the same yesterday, today, and forever. He sees the end from the beginning, and still, His Word says what it says. It was just as true centuries ago as it is today. It will still be true tomorrow, and next week, and many years from now.

This is why we stake every facet of our lives on the Word of God. It is a firm foundation, abundant in promises, with an answer for every question all the days of our lives.

I encourage you to take these next seven days to look afresh into God's Word. In these pages, you will see God repeatedly intervene in impossible situations. These aren't just stories. These accounts are truth, and they bring life and refreshing. Approach this 7-day journey with your faith active and open to receive God's promise.

May these next seven days restore your hope, build your faith, and stir your expectation. It's time to receive *The Joyful Mother Promise*.

DAY ONE

The Promise is Yes and Amen

The promises of God are unchanging. What He has done for one, He will do for another. This means that everything we find in His Word, we can take personally.

> For all the promises of God in Him are Yes, and in Him Amen, to the glory of God through us.
>
> —2 Corinthians 1:20

Isn't that refreshing? Isn't that comforting? *All* the promises are yes and amen. Not one is in question, as far as the Lord is concerned.

> He maketh the barren woman to keep house, and to be a joyful mother of children. Praise ye the Lord.
> —Psalm 113:9 (KJV)

This *Joyful Mother Promise* from God is yes and amen. It is no mistake that the Lord makes mention of "the barren woman" in the first part of that sentence. That which is supposed to be physically impossible, that which is supposed to be hopeless in the natural—*it is well*, with God.

> For with God nothing shall be impossible.
> —Luke 1:37 (KJV)

Declare this: "I am a joyful mother of children. God has said it, I believe Him, so it is so in my life."

Now, thank Him and praise Him for His Word—which is *true*—and this miracle the Lord has ordained for your life!

One powerful tool the Lord has given you to stir up and energize your faith is your imagination. When you imagine something dreadful, your emotions, body, and thoughts all participate in that imagination. Yet, when your imagination is in alignment with faith in God's Word, your emotions, body, and thoughts all participate in that instead.

Picture your life as a mother, narrowing in on things that spark joy. Maybe for you, the picture is a messy-hair day with a pile of laundry and extra dishes in the kitchen sink, because all of that means your house is *fuller* and your family has *grown*. Or maybe, the picture is of you holding one of your babies, singing to them, and seeing their little fingers wrap around one of yours.

Keep a joy-sparking imagination directed at this *Joyful Mother Promise* daily. Everything in you responds to what you focus on.

TODAY'S REFLECTION QUESTIONS:
1. Are you excited about this *Joyful Mother Promise*? Is this real to you?
2. As you imagine stepping into the fullness of this precious promise, do you feel the joy of the Lord?

Rebekah's miracle
is a simple picture
of God's response
to the
prayer of faith.

DAY TWO

Rebekah

When Prayer Opens the Womb

> Isaac was forty years old when he married Rebekah... And Isaac prayed much to the Lord for his wife because she was unable to bear children; and the Lord granted his prayer, and Rebekah his wife became pregnant.
>
> —Genesis 25:20–21 (AMPC)

Rebekah was unable to have children, but her husband prayed to the Lord on her behalf. What a gift for a wife to have a husband who prays for her!

It's not a prerequisite to receive this miracle of the *Joyful Mother Promise*, but this example is particularly helpful to highlight for three reasons:

1. Rebekah was barren, but she became a mother with children. Trust in God: You *shall* conceive, you *shall* carry, and you *shall* bear and behold your babies.

2. Some women carry guilt, shame, and heaviness over fertility struggles or barrenness. If that's you, reject those things; they are not from God, and they do not cooperate with faith. Rebekah's miracle is a simple picture of God's response to the prayer of faith.

3. According to Scripture, this miracle was in response to Isaac's prayer, which demonstrates that God's response is not limited to the woman's level of faith or her prayers. Women are not necessarily solely responsible (spiritually) for stepping into this miracle from God.

> I sought the Lord, and he heard me, and delivered me from all my fears.
>
> —Psalm 34:4 (KJV)

> For the eyes of the Lord are over the righteous, and his ears are open unto their prayers.
>
> —1 PETER 3:12A (KJV)

The Lord hears you when you call! He is not deaf or hard of hearing. He is not ignoring you, forgetting you, or withholding from you. He is *faithful* to deliver you from whatever stands between you and your miracle.

Declare this: "I am a joyful mother of children. God has said it, I believe Him, so it is so in my life."

Now, thank Him and praise Him for His faithfulness and the grace to see the manifestation of this miracle!

TODAY'S REFLECTION QUESTIONS:

1. What is one scripture you are standing on to build your faith for receiving the *Joyful Mother Promise*? Confess and declare it daily, using it as an anchor for your faith and expectation.

2. Are you daily talking to the Lord about this desire of your heart, making room for Him to comfort you, encourage you, and grace you to receive His best for you?

The Lord
remembered
Hannah and
she conceived.

DAY THREE

Hannah

The Cry of the Heart

Hannah grieved the absence of children she desired. Her longing was deep and sorrowful. She was mocked by her husband's other wife. Hannah felt humiliated and desperate.

Isaac prayed for Rebekah and her womb, but Hannah's husband was bothered by her deep desire for children.

Then Elkanah her husband said to her,

> Hannah, why do you cry? And why do you
> not eat? And why are you grieving? Am I
> not more to you than ten sons?
> —1 Samuel 1:8 (AMPC)

Hannah didn't have the support, compassion, or agreement of her husband in this area of her life. The Bible doesn't say she showed him dishonor or disrespect for his attitude toward her and her situation, but she did not give up this desire of her heart either.

> [Hannah] was in bitterness of soul, and prayed to the Lord and wept in anguish. Then she made a vow and said, "O Lord of hosts, if You will indeed look on the affliction of Your maidservant and remember me, and not forget Your maidservant, but will give Your maidservant a male child, then I will give him to the Lord all the days of his life..."
> —1 Samuel 1:10–11

Something was different with this particular prayer: she made a vow, commanding the attention of Heaven.

Eli, the priest, saw Hannah as she petitioned

the Lord. He thought she was drunk, but Hannah replied:

> "No, my lord, I am a woman of sorrowful spirit. I have drunk neither wine nor intoxicating drink, but have poured out my soul before the Lord."
>
> —1 SAMUEL 1:15

Eli told her to go in peace and expect the Lord to grant her petition. She got up and was no longer sad. As you continue reading in 1 Samuel 1, you see the Lord remembered Hannah and she conceived. She gave glory to the Lord for the miracle and honored her vow.

> For there is no respect of persons with God.
>
> —ROMANS 2:11 (KJV)

God has no partiality, no favoritism toward people, but He *is* a respecter of faith. Since God responded directly to the cry of Hannah's heart, petition, and faith, He will do the same for *you*. When other women around you are having their babies, remember Hannah was in the same position—and God came through for her!

Declare this: "I am a joyful mother of children. God has said it, I believe Him, so it is so in my life." Now, praise Him for the victory!

TODAY'S REFLECTION QUESTIONS:
1. Do you have confidence in your heart that God is with you, showing no partiality to others that He is withholding from you? If not, declare scriptures daily that firmly root this truth in your heart.
2. Have you petitioned the Lord from a place of desperation, pure motive, and wholehearted honesty?

DAY FOUR

Sarah

When the Body Says Impossible

In your physical body, as a result of natural aging or something out of order, a doctor may say it is impossible for you to conceive or carry a baby to full term.

When things of this natural realm come against the divine truth found in the Word of God, you must be *unshakable*, unaccepting of anything that contradicts God and His plan.

> Is anything too hard for the Lord?
> —Genesis 18:14

The Lord asked Abraham if anything is too hard for Him, because Sarah laughed at the promise of a son coming forth from her womb in old age. If you laugh in response to God's promise, be sure you are laughing from His joy and not from unbelief or doubt!

Sarah's situation was physically impossible. Yet, the word of the Lord was spoken, and the miracle was set in motion. You must realize that the *moment* the word of the Lord comes, whether through a scripture you read or what the Lord has spoken to your heart, the miracle is set in motion! It's the planting of a seed that is designed to spring up with new life and purpose.

> By faith Sarah herself also received strength to conceive seed, and she bore a child when she was past the age, because she judged Him faithful who had promised.
> —Hebrews 11:11

He is faithful! In His Word, He has promised you shall be a joyful mother of children, and He is *faithful.*

Declare this: "I am a joyful mother of children. God has said it, I believe Him, so it is so in my life."

Now, give Him thanks and glory for His provision, His promise, and His faithfulness!

TODAY'S REFLECTION QUESTIONS:

1. Do you wholeheartedly judge God faithful, as Sarah did? Could you press for deeper revelation of His faithfulness, overflowing your joy tank and accelerating your breakthrough?
2. Do you recognize the supreme authority of God over all creation and all circumstances?

Nothing is
impossible with
God, and *all things*
are possible to
those who believe!

DAY FIVE

Elizabeth

Nothing is Impossible

Much like Sarah, Elizabeth was past the age of childbearing and her situation was physically impossible. What the Lord did in the Old Testament, He also did in the New Testament. He is still doing this *today*!

Luke 1 is an absolutely incredible chapter in the Bible. Two miracle babies are conceived. If you need to stir up your faith for miraculous conception, read this chapter on repeat.

Elizabeth conceived in her old age, just as the

angel of the Lord had spoken to Zacharias, her husband. When an angel came to Mary and spoke of her miraculous conception of Jesus, the angel also said:

> "Now indeed, Elizabeth your relative has also conceived a son in her old age; and this is now the sixth month for her who was called barren. For with God nothing will be impossible."
>
> –LUKE 1:36–37

At the onset of one miraculous conception, was the announcement of another that had taken place six months prior. "She who was *barren* is now *six months along*." Why? "With God *nothing* will be impossible."

Luke 1:24–25 says Elizabeth hid herself for five months after conceiving. This was such a precious miracle, and she knew she was seen personally by the Lord. This was holy.

We must be like Elizabeth in Luke 1:25, giving glory and honor to the Lord. We must be like Mary in Luke 1:38 and say to the Lord, "Let it be to me according to Your Word."

Declare this: "I am a joyful mother of children. God has said it, I believe Him, so it is so in my life.

Lord, let it be to me according to Your Word!"

Now, rejoice, because *nothing* is impossible with God, and *all things* are possible to those who believe!

TODAY'S REFLECTION QUESTIONS:
1. Can you feel faith stirring up and growing this week as you plant these seeds of the Word of God into your heart? The praise you give Him daily is watering these seeds.
2. Are you inviting the presence of God to flood your heart and life as you read Luke 1? In His presence is fullness of *joy*!

Your spoken words
are important!
Discretion makes
way for a miracle.

DAY SIX

The Shunammite Woman

Faith Refuses Defeat

The Shunammite woman's account is found in 2 Kings 4. Scripture calls her a notable woman. She desired to bless and honor the prophet Elisha.

As a result of her hospitality and generosity, the prophet was compelled to see her blessed. Gehazi, Elisha's servant, told Elisha that she had no son and her husband was old.

> So he said, "Call her." When he had called her, she stood in the doorway. Then he said, "About this time next year you shall

> embrace a son." And she said, "No, my lord. Man of God, do not lie to your maidservant!"
>
> —2 KINGS 4:15–16

Such vulnerability in her response! The prophet had located a *deep* desire of her heart, tender and hidden.

Just as the prophet had spoken, the woman miraculously bore a son at the appointed time. God *saw* her, and her generosity commanded the blessing of Heaven upon her life.

A couple verses later, this miracle child died in her lap. She didn't fret, mourn, or even tell her husband their son had died.

> Then she called to her husband, and said, "Please send me one of the young men and one of the donkeys, that I may run to the man of God and come back." So he said, "Why are you going to him today?" ... And she said, "It is well."
>
> —2 KINGS 4:22–23

In the face of death, she took a bold position of unshakable faith. She set out to meet Elisha. When Gehazi approached her, she simply said again: "It is well" (v 26).

> Now when she came to the man of God
> at the hill, she caught him by the feet, but
> Gehazi came near to push her away. But
> the man of God said, "Let her alone; for
> her soul is in deep distress, and the Lord
> has hidden it from me, and has not told
> me." So she said, "Did I ask a son of my
> lord? Did I not say, 'Do not deceive me'?"
>
> —2 KINGS 4:27–28

She would not tell anyone what had happened, not even Elisha. Notice she questions him, but she does not declare death has taken her son. Your spoken words are important! Discretion makes way for a miracle.

Elisha went to the dead child and did as he was led by the Lord.

> ...the child opened his eyes. And [Elisha]
> called Gehazi and said, "Call this
> Shunammite woman." So he called her.
> And when she came in to him, he said,
> "Pick up your son." So she went in, fell at
> his feet, and bowed to the ground; then she
> picked up her son and went out.
>
> —2 KINGS 4:35–37

She couldn't have a child, but she bore one at the word of the Lord. Her miracle child died, but he was resurrected by the power of God.

Declare this: "I am a joyful mother of children. God has said it, I believe Him, so it is so in my life. It is WELL!"

Praise Him, woman of God! Magnify His Name, and recall He has placed His Word above His Name (Psalm 138:2). This promise is for *you*!

TODAY'S REFLECTION QUESTIONS:

1. Do you realize that truly *nothing* is impossible for God, and that truly *all things* are possible as you believe Him?

2. Can you picture the Shunammite woman as she walked out these events? Receive an impartation of discretion, boldness, and confidence in God; be encouraged by her example.

DAY SEVEN
God Hasn't Changed His Mind

Rebekah, Hannah, Sarah, Elizabeth, and the Shunammite woman were each in circumstances where they couldn't have children. But God!

The same miracles He worked in their lives and in their wombs, He will work in *your* life and in *your* womb. You must make the decision that you directly and personally have what He's said in His Word. From that decision, you *speak* the words that align with His promises and your faith, and you *don't speak* the words that come against your miracle.

> Death and life are in the power of the tongue...
>
> —PROVERBS 18:21

Speak life! Speak blessing. Your words must line up with His Word.

> Do not be deceived, God is not mocked; for whatever a man sows, that he will also reap. And let us not grow weary while doing good, for in due season we shall reap if we do not lose heart.
>
> —GALATIANS 6:7,9

Whatever you sow, you're going to reap. Whatever you speak, you're going to have.

> Let us hold fast the confession of our hope without wavering, for He who promised is faithful.
>
> —HEBREWS 10:23

God is faithful. *Everything* He says is true. You can stake your life on every word He has spoken. You mustn't waver!

> God is not a man, that He should lie, nor a son of man, that He should repent. Has He said, and will He not do? Or has He spoken, and will He not make it good?
>
> —NUMBERS 23:19

But the Lord is the true God; He is the living God and the everlasting King...
>
> —JEREMIAH 10:10

The path to *guaranteed victory*:
- Know what God has said
- Know He is trustworthy and faithful
- Take Him at His Word and believe Him
- Speak only that which aligns with your faith and His promises

When you follow God's plan and obey His Word, your victory is guaranteed. Every opposition must bow to the authority of God and His Word. As you cooperate with His plan and obey His Word, you cannot be defeated, and you *shall* have that which you petition Him for.

> He maketh the barren woman to keep house, and to be a joyful mother of children. Praise ye the Lord.
>
> —PSALM 113:9 (KJV)

Declare this: "I am a joyful mother of children. God has said it, I believe Him, so it is so in my life. Because I cooperate with and participate in the plan of God for my life, I shall have victory!"

Give Him glory, for He's worthy of all your praise! Rejoice with a praise that costs you, a sacrificial offering that demonstrates your faith and confidence in your Heavenly Father. Hallelujah!

TODAY'S REFLECTION QUESTIONS:
1. Are your words lining up with your faith and God's promises? Are there any words you are speaking that are working against your miracle?
2. Are you fully cooperating with and wholeheartedly participating—spirit, soul, and body—in God's plan for you to be a joyful mother of children? Ask the Lord to show you any areas needing adjustments, with clear instructions, and follow His leading.

A FINAL WORD

These seven days are not meant to be rushed through and left behind.

Return as needed. Revisit what God has spoken.

Let His Word settle, take root, and bring forth what He has promised.

> Rooted and built up in Him and established in the faith…
>
> —Colossians 2:7

> For the word of God is living and powerful…
>
> —Hebrews 4:12

NOTES

NOTES

POSTSCRIPT

It has been a pleasure to navigate this week with you in *The Joyful Mother Promise*, looking to God and His Word for truths you can apply to any opposition you face as you endeavor to have children. He is with you and for you; He has promised to never leave you or forsake you, but rather to be your very present help in time of need.

If this book has blessed you, you can contact us at novaseipress.com to share your testimony. We'd love to hear from and rejoice with you.

If you desire to see others find these seven days of simple but significant seeds of faith, you can write a review on Amazon or Goodreads, send a copy of this book to someone else, or share about your experience on social media.

Lastly, if you'd like to continue this journey, join me for a deeper dive with my book, *Called to Motherhood: Trusting God Beyond Fear, Grief, and Delay*. I would love to share the rest of this message with you, imparting what I've learned, so that you have access to these keys the Lord has given me. What He has done for one, He will do for all. He is faithful.

Thank you for being here. I pray these pages transform your life beyond what you could have asked, thought, or imagined, as you apply the teachings within.

ABOUT THE AUTHOR

Elizabeth Wilson is the founder of Nova Sei Press, a publishing house committed to releasing Christian-authored books with excellence and helping self-publishing writers bring their projects to life with clarity and care. She studied at River University in Tampa, Florida, where her love for Scripture and ministry deepened.

Elizabeth lives in Tennessee with her husband and daughter. Her writing reflects her heart to encourage believers to live surrendered, rooted in truth, and confident in God's strength.

Other books by Elizabeth Wilson:

Before You Give Up: A 7-Day Devotional

Just Give Up! When Striving Gives Way to God's Strength

Called to Motherhood: Trusting God Beyond Fear, Grief, and Delay

NOVA SEI PRESS

Nova Sei Press exists to publish Christian-authored books with excellence and to support independent authors through thoughtful, professional publishing services. With a focus on integrity, craftsmanship, and faithfulness to Scripture, Nova Sei Press seeks to steward words that strengthen the Church and serve readers well.

Connect with Nova Sei Press on Instagram, Facebook, and YouTube: @novaseipress.

SEEDS OF SIGNIFICANCE

Seeds of Significance is a series of seven-day devotionals designed to plant biblical truth in everyday life. Each book offers short, Scripture-centered readings that take about five minutes a day, making it simple to stay rooted in God's Word even in a full season of life. This volume is the second in the series.

Before You Give Up, the first volume, invites you to cultivate steady faith through consistent, daily surrender.

The next volume in the series, *Gather Not A Few*, stirs up your faith expectation for God to do what He said He would do.

SALVATION

As you have been reading this book, maybe the Lord has been tugging at your heart in light of eternity. Yes, we have this life to live on the Earth, but then the Lord's plan is for Heaven to be our home in eternity, not the devil's Hell.

If you fit into any of the three categories below, I'm inviting you to pray now.
- You don't know for sure if you are on your way to Heaven.
- You haven't received Jesus into your heart as your personal Lord and Savior.
- You want to make a fresh commitment to the Lord and be confident that you are in right standing with Him.

Pray this prayer, and mean it in your heart as you speak the words out loud:

Father, I come to You in the precious Name of Your Son, Jesus. You said in Your Word, if I confess with my mouth and believe in my heart, that I will be saved. Forgive me of my sins. Wash me and cleanse me. Set me free. Jesus, I believe that You're risen from the dead, and You're coming back again for me. I forgive anyone who has ever hurt me, and I forgive myself. I'm saved, I'm born again, I'm forgiven, and I'm set free. Thank You, Lord, for saving me now. Give me a passion for the lost, a hunger for the things of God, and a holy boldness to preach the Gospel of Jesus Christ. I love You, Lord. In Jesus' Name, I pray. Amen.

As a minister of the Gospel of Jesus Christ, I tell you today that your sins are forgiven you right now. Always remember to run to God and not from Him, because He loves you and has a wonderful plan for your life.